FIRST
KATHA BOOK
of haiku, senryu, tanka & haibun

edited by kala ramesh, johannes manjrekar and vidur jyoti
afterword by tracy koretsky

art by surabhi singh

CONTENTS

preface

by kala ramesh

It is a proud moment for us, as we can lay claim to the fact that this was the first e-book to be published in 2013, and now, in a print edition, it remains the FIRST Katha book of haiku, senryu, tanka and haibun to come from India. Rabindranath Tagore and Subramania Bharati were the pioneers of haiku in our country. Although we've always had poets from regional languages exploring haiku in all its nuances, it has been centred on a nucleus largely unknown to the wider world.

The publication of FIRST in a print edition for young adults gains further importance when we realize that India, which draws so much sustenance from nature and her transient seasons, has begun to explore this addictive English-language haiku in a big way. The last decade has seen a Himalayan-rise in the popularity of haikai literature in our country and the haikai world has begun to take notice!

In this anthology, which was collated in 2009, we have thirty-five poets' work represented in haiku and allied genres such as senryu, tanka and haibun. Each of these genres is a specialised form of writing. Ironically, haiku, which is concise, brief and over in few words, is subject to many norms and conventions. Nevertheless, haiku emphasises simplicity. What is striking is its imagery, showing us the creative force of nature, ever-changing and transient.

Haiku is also called "the wordless poem", meaning the words are so simple that they seem to drop away, and what's left behind is just the image, clearly etched in the reader's mind. There is a saying, "when you point to the moon with your bejewelled hand, all I see is your hand."

All these genres employ the strategy of showing rather than telling.

Rasa

an artiste is one
who
with a glance
a flicker of a smile
a hand gesture
or that feel in her voice
brings out the rasa
an artiste is true
when
with just a hint here
a trace there
she allows the rasa to bloom
and, anything less is truly more ...[1]

The subtle art of suggestion is what makes these genres so enthralling. The capacity to understand navarasa[2] is ingrained in most of us, as is abhinaya[3]. Indian artists have been working on these principles for a very long time. When we read about the lateral space or the semi-circle in haiku, or about the "dreaming room" that is so essential to these art forms, we instinctively know what it implies: making room for the reader / a rasika, to step in.

[1] *Rasa* – free verse poem by Kala Ramesh
[2] *navarasa* – the nine rasas of the Ancient Indian theory of art
[3] *abhinaya* – art of subtle suggestion as against drama

haiku

a thiagarajan

autumn evening
I lightly touch
my son's first scribbles

autumn evening – The Heron's Nest VIII, 2, 2006

haiku

mid-may
the narielwala walks across
for a cold coke

road puddles —
the umbrellas dip
at each passing car

almost evening —
the paper vendor sleeps
on old news

mid may – DNA Mumbai, February 25, 2006
road puddles – The Heron's Nest VIII, 4, 2006
almost evening – The Heron's Nest, March 2008

amitava dasgupta

pain fades
through the hospital window
cherry blossoms

haiku

angelee deodhar

rumours of war
up into a darkening sky
— a child's newsprint kite

over the lake ...
a wagtail dips into
ripples of mist

only their eyes ...
buffaloes swim through
the rain swollen river

rumours of war – Third Prize, The Robert Spiess Memorial Haiku Award, 2003

muted rain song ...
from the verandah eaves
the drip of droplets

clumps of snow
cling to tree hollows
raw spring breeze

late for school
the green mangoes still
out of reach

haiku

at the exit gate
arrested by a shock
of sunflowers

fading into the tan
of her shoulder
a tattooed butterfly

a light breeze
the moon in the birdbath
shivers

sharing an umbrella
your wet left shoulder
my right one

winter
shaken away, in the wag
of a duck's tail

acres of darkness
outside, inside
then a firefly

sharing an umbrella – Pail in Hand, 2000

haiku

a sethuramiah

between me
and the mountain range
a train passes

between me – Mainichi Daily news, July 2009

bhavani ramesh

winter evening ...
the roadside chaiwala
makes more money

spring cleaning
I stack away my memories
in the cupboard

sidewalk café
I smell the city
in my coffee

winter eve – World Haiku Review, March 2008
spring cleaning – Part of a renku in Thanal, Online, September 2008
sidewalk café – Chrysanthemums, April 2008

haiku

charishma ramchandani

the full moon
bowing between bamboo —
sudden storm

new year's eve ...
in my wine glass
two lovers kiss

chitra rajappa

thunderclap —
the sleeping newborn
throws up her arms

thunderclap – Chrysanthemums, April 2008

haiku

devika menon

winter evening
the rock garden
wrapped in wind

summer sunset —
   the chai-seller
flicks ash on the beach

first anniversary dinner ...
only the cilantro
fresh

g s p rao

autumn deepens ...
the tree releases a leaf
into ballet

haiku

gautam nadkarni

sudden rain —
umbrellas mushroom
on the street

ganeshotsav
waves of devotees
immerse the god

church graveyard —
from somewhere close
the fragrance of lilies

sultry noon —
the cold sherbet hawker
drinks water

diwali night ...
the new year begins
with old folk tales

sudden rain – Shiki kukai, 1st prize, May 2009
church graveyard – The Heron's Nest, March 2009

haiku

neighbour's tree
its shade on my side
of the wall

winter dusk —
the old man's emails
finally stop coming

neighbour's tree – World Haiku Review, March 2008
winter dusk – Modern Haiku, Autumn 2008

harish suryanarayana

still winter night
the wind chimes tinkle
as I close the door

still winter night – World Haiku Review, April 2008

haiku

johannes manjrekar

night walk
I slow down
near the jasmine bush

stalled traffic
a cow picks flowers
off the wedding car

rumble of thunder
a sunbird comes darting
through the wire fence

petal strewn ground
a mynah hops into
a patch of light

funeral procession
a bee lands on the flowers

declining moon
the old man's laughter
turns to coughing

night walk – Temps Libres, 2005
stalled traffic – Temps Libres, February 2009
funeral procession – Temps Libres, February 2009
declining moon – Temps Libres, February 2009

haiku

kala ramesh

the pause
in a dragonfly's glide —
noon shadows

dense fog ...
the train evaporates
into a distant horn

the pause – Tinywords, May 2008
dense fog – The Heron's Nest, June 2009

autumn chill
the ashtray holds
their conversation

kite contest
     the rise and fall
of oohs and aahs

liquid twilight
the tilt of a water pot
on her hip

autumn chill – Presence Haiku Journal # 39, 2013
kite contest – Moonset, The newspaper, Spring 2010
liquid twilight – Frogpond, Fall 2008

haiku

k ramesh

vedic chants ...
a heron glides to a rock
in the misty lake

meditation over ...
the full moon
between the branches

vedic chants – The Heron's Nest, Vol X, No 2, June 2008

sound of waves
a jogger stops to watch
the fishermen leave

emptying my bag ...
the pebble makes me
think of the hill again

rural school —
the shy smiles of children
waiting for the bus

emptying my bag – The Heron's Nest, Vol XI, No 1, March 2009
rural school – The Heron's Nest, Vol X, No 1, March 2008

haiku

drift of a leaf ...
students pray in silence
in the courtyard

drift of a leaf – Presence Haiku Journal # 38, 2009

kameshwar rao

pacing my steps
to a bird's morning call

pacing my steps – Chrysanthemum, April 2008

haiku

kumarendra mallick

morning walk —
the children cycle
over my shadow

summer camp ...
my child paints
a winter landscape

autumn morning —
my shadow now
has a slight hunch

summer clouds —
an umbrella for the hawker
selling greens

autumn shadow – World Haiku Review, Spring 2009
summer clouds – World Haiku Review, Spring 2009

haiku

minal sarosh

empty days ...
my old bones creak
with the swing

n k singh

tides wash away
the sands of Puri
and our body prints

autumn ...
leaves tumble into
a painter's palette

faded days —
why do old ponds stir
muddy memories?

haiku

narendra kumar dixit

heavy downpour ...
through the trembling leaves
a flash of lightning

puja malushte

old bridge
the song of a bird
passes through

evening sun
my shadow enters
through the door

autumn dusk
just the two of us
me and my waiting

twilight
between you and me
the moon

haiku

purushothama rao

spring rain ...
the tree and I
in conversation

r j kalpana

high noon —
by the car a girl stands
on her shadow

floundering boat
a river fog curls
around my ankles

first sailboat —
I stretch my hand
to split waves

haiku

r k singh

Making lemon tea
and warm buttery toast —
birds singing outside

Hanging
by a spider's thread —
the wanton leaf

Her fingers push
the roots into the earth —
touch-me-not

raju samal

bored in heaven
a shooting star
jumps to death

flood of dawn ...
the morning star
sinks

bored in heaven – World Haiku Review, April 2008
flood of dawn – Chrysanthemum, April 2008

haiku

rohini gupta

cloud shadows —
drifting across the valley
field by field

temple ruins
only the wind still
offers flowers

light rain
the red rose
overflows

vacations end
my small black notebook
brings home the mountains

dawn comes
too soon
I lose the stars

temple ruins – Chrysanthemums, April 2008
light rain – The Heron's Nest, June 2008
vacations end – Bottlerockets, August 2008
dawn comes – Bottlerockets, February 2009

haiku

s b vadivelrajan

summer evening —
a crab races
with the beach wave

waterfall ...
searching for my breath
in the biting chill

seshu chamarty

the eclipsed sun
emerges from darkness
my alarm rings

haiku

srinjay chakravarti

shaded garden
a golden flash
of an oriole's wings

monsoon clouds ...
a herd of water buffalo
wades into the pond

sunil uniyal

parched field —
a tattered scarecrow
still on vigil

on a night train —
glow-worms outside
catch my eyes

country drive —
the one-legged scarecrow
heckled by sparrows

the mist is heavy
having swallowed all mountains
and paddy fields

on a night train – Notes From the Gean, June 2009
country drive – Notes From the Gean, June 2009
the mist is heavy – Notes From the Gean, June 2009

haiku

usha kiran

slow traffic
a vilambit teen taal
on my radio

slow traffic – World Haiku Review, April 2008

power cut …
today I hear
the birds chirp

running to catch my bus
I almost miss
the sunset

leaving home
sitting in my favourite chair
a wee bit longer

haiku

vidur jyoti

first rains ...
I let go of my umbrella
to hold her hand

your breath
on the glass pane
a bit of frost

rain dancing ...
swirling clouds scatter
the moonbeams

vishnu p kapoor

placid lake —
a frisky frog sinks
the full moon

wishing well —
the treasure trove of coins
and a few frogs

early thaw
her hand brushes mine
under the quilt

early thaw – Tinywords, January 2007

haiku

senryu

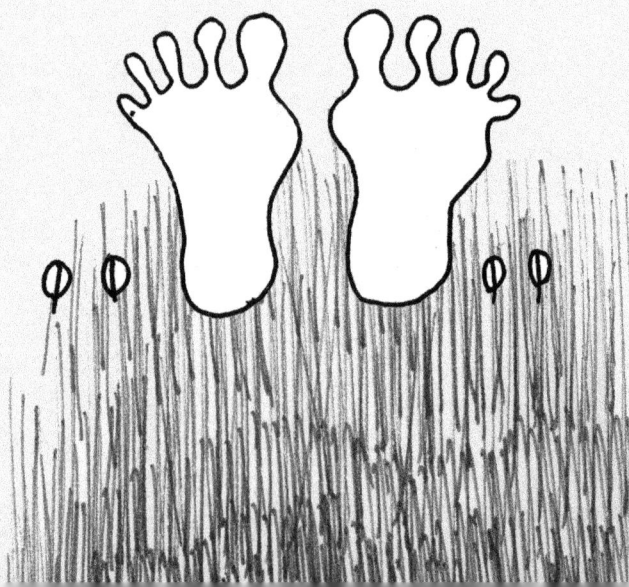

a thiagarajan

house hunt —
our dog inspects
all corners

yoga class ...
the child looks at her mom
upside down

"men are scum"
she says
divorcing a third time

househunt – The Heron's Nest XI, 2, 2009
yoga class – White Lotus, Issue 3, 2006
men are scum – Simply Haiku, Summer 2009

senryu

devika menon

twelfth birthday —
the butcher's daughter
turns vegan

gautam nadkarni

adventure beckons ...
I go camping in the
backyard

smiling back I find
that the girl is smiling
at someone else

after the family photo
mom removes
her dentures

he hesitates
to say he is hungry,
the stepson

adventure beckons – Simply Haiku, Winter 2007
smiling back I find (variation) – Simply Haiku, Winter 2008
after the family photo – Simply Haiku, Winter 2008
he hesitates – Simply Haiku, Spring 2008

senryu

johannes manjrekar

orthopaedic clinic
a three-legged chair
outside the entrance

traffic argument
the camel's sneer
is impartial

burnt house
the owner's name
on the iron gate

smell of newsprint
twenty beauty queens
with one smile

orthopaedic clinic – Temps Libres, March 2004
traffic argument – Temps Libres, February 2004
burnt house – Temps Libres, March 2003
smell of newsprint – Temps Libres, January 2002

senryu

kala ramesh

circus clown ...
show over, he pulls off
his painted smile

circus clown – 3 Lights Gallery, Spring 2009

kumarendra mallick

weekend outing
the newly wed
packs her dreams

senryu

reshma jain

blurry sonograph ...
she is insecure
even in the womb

blurry sonograph – World Haiku Review, April 2008

seshu chamarty

ghost movie
watched it again
in my dream

senryu

srinjay chakravarti

barber's saloon:
the morse code
of clicking scissors

sunil uniyal

delhi red fort —
the guide twirls his
moustache
talking of shah jahan

senryu

usha kiran

lazy afternoon ...
he gives me directions
as I scratch his back

toilet ...
smell of freshly fried papad
from our neighbour's kitchen

vishnu p kapoor

morning peace
vanishes with the arrival
of my newspaper

senryu

tanka

a thiagarajan

for each om
an inhale and an exhale
counting the holds
with an ear on the doorbell
for the morning milk

for each om – Eucalypt, Issue 6, 2009

tanka

kala ramesh

the crow
sweeps in like an eagle
I discover
I *do* do things
like my mother

longing
for more, I linger ...
a quiet breath
over the widening blue
of sea and sky

the crow – Eucalypt, Issue 6, 2009

I gather
one moon after
another
into my hands ...
the river keeps giving

laughing
over old stories ...
suddenly
I feel that mother
is young again

I gather – Ribbons Tanka Society's Journal, March 2008
laughing over old stories – Gean Tree Press #2, 2009

tanka

k ramesh

getting up early
to catch the morning train,
I am in the backyard now
in the presence
of stars

one more
bomb blast ...
morning drizzle
falls on
the newspaper

september night ...
correcting papers,
I notice an upside down
beetle turning over
on its own

purple dawn ...
I wake up to
the slight movement
of her fingers in
my hand

the kitten and I
stand silently
at the door
watching the darkness
settle among the trees

summer evening —
no train to catch,
two old men chat
sitting on the bench
of this small station

searching for coins
in my pocket —
red seeds
collected by
my little daughter

september night – Tanka Splendor Award 2005
the kitten and I – Lynx XVIII:3, October 2003
summer evening – Tanka Splendor Award 2002
searching for coins – American Tanka, October 2001

tanka

r k singh

Awaiting the waves
that'll wash away empty hours
and endless longing
in this dead silence at sea
I pull down chunks of sky

Awaiting the waves – Lynx XXI:2, June 2006

shernaz wadia

silver fish
have burrowed through
my past
I burn the old diary
with pages full of you

I roam these hills
in wonder ...
each step
each breath
becomes a prayer

this glassy lake
of tranquillity ...
sitting at its edge
with one breath
I swallow the universe

silver fish – Atlas Poetica, Issue 4, 2009
this glassy lake – Ribbons, June 2008

tanka

vidur jyoti

winter sun
in the bare branches
a kite sways
as shadows lengthen
she lights a lamp

all words
collected from silence
and their shadows
born of light
so heavy, this baggage

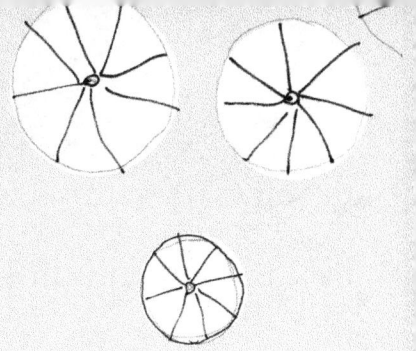

haibun

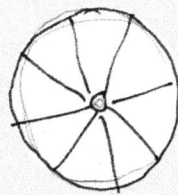

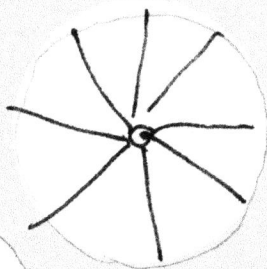

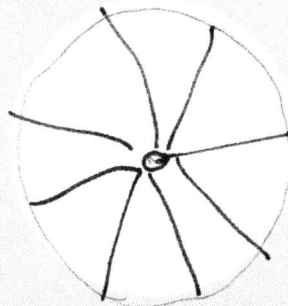

aju mukhopadhyay

Crickets Drone

Of our many pets, guests and visitors, the latest are the crickets. Droning of crickets we often hear, especially in the evenings in the countryside. Our town suddenly turned warm this spring and some crickets had taken shelter in our bathroom, toilet and storeroom — places less frequented by humans.

Just as the darkness falls, they begin droning in unison. It goes on till morning. As I enter their rooms and ask, "Oh, who's making such loud calls?" They pause, only to resume after a while. I have seen two of them in action: mouths are shut but their rear wings flutter rhythmically with the drone.

early spring
a rangoon creeper shamelessly blooms
day in and day out

johannes manjrekar

Evening

The sun has set and darkness — is it really descending, settling on the earth the way poets and songwriters tell us? On this hot evening it seems more like a vapour rising from the baking earth, making its escape from gravity as soon as the sun is no longer watching ...

Shapes are still discernible, and a bit of colour. The little boy — I can't make out his features, but going by size he's maybe three years old — is wearing a red shirt and nothing else. The girl beside him is maybe two years older, probably his sister. They are sitting on a straw mat in front of the nearest hut outside my garden. Voices from the little colony of migrant workers come filtering through the wire fence, punctuating the evening silence. Suddenly the boy begins to laugh, a clear gurgling laugh that keeps tripping over itself. The girl joins in, but her laughter is more restrained. After all, she is the elder one.

easter moon —
smoke rises
from the cooking fire

haibun

Magisterial

I was about eight when I decided that my favourite word was "triumph". Not for its meaning — I merely loved the sound of it, pronounced the German way. Tree-oomph. It seemed to rev up in your throat before being propelled out with a little extra push at the end. And there was a car too named Triumph — Triumph Spitfire — wasn't there? I possessed a card game, a different car on each card, that I played with my uncle. We would draw a card each and see who had the higher horsepower, top speed and so forth. One time we fell out over the rules for rating cars, and after that we never played the card game again. I guess he too wasn't completely grown up then, my uncle. He wasn't even forty.

I'm older than that now, and thought I'd outgrown this childish fancy for the sound of a word. But suddenly I find that I love the word "magisterial", entirely without loving magistrates or magisterial demeanour, or any of the baggage that words have come to carry at this age. Perhaps it's because of the bare tree full of crows that I saw against a grey sky.

monsoon clouds
crow silhouettes complete
the leafless tree

Change

Saturday evening. Tired and hungry, I'm eating a puff at the roadside tea stall. A young boy comes up to beg, his younger sister in tow. One or two rupees, he says. His sister says nothing, merely stares at me wide-eyed.
I have no loose change. Before I can tell the boy so, he pats the pocket of his ragged shorts. I have change, he says half proudly, half smiling. I can change you a tenner. Even fifteen rupees.

evening moon
I wipe my glasses
all over again

evening – Temps Libre, April 2009
magisterial – Temps Libre, June 2009 and Haibun Today, Vol. 5,w No. 1, 2011

haibun

kala ramesh

The Threshold

distant rapids ...
a rumbling song
from the bridge

"Suicide point," the guide says, "you need to see it, Memsahib." The driver takes the car up the mountain range, without grace or expertise, it looks like he'll kill us even before we reach this Suicide Point. Up and up we go through raw muddy roads. The car comes mercifully to a halt. We walk toward the famed point and look ...

Down
Sheer fall
A single sheet of dripping mist, almost pulls the sky into the valley. And from beyond the horizon a reddish-orange glow softly spreads ... the beginnings of another day.

wind
    my hair
in your face

the threshold – contemporary haibun online, March 2009

r j kalpana

Mentor

I thought she had it all; a shelf full of classics, friends to laugh with, a spray of water to tickle her toes. All those soirees we attended late evenings, hotly discussing the latest verse to catch our fancy, or the turn of a phrase that heated our blood. When did it all get too much for her that she had to just end it? Late one evening, I walk across her silent house once again.

broken shutters —
the summer moon
squinting through

haibun

vidur jyoti

Are You There?

Why is sleep so elusive?
Just like the clock on the wall am I also destined to stay awake? Even
tonight, the stark stillness resounds with footfalls of *time* — turning around I
confront only myself, with *time* hiding behind the calendar on the wall and
tugging at the clock.

Moonbeams, at times sunrays too, peep through the window — the floral
pattern of the grill breaks the beams into millions of shafts which pierce my
loneliness. There is so much pain in that pleasure.
Why would I fall asleep, tonight?

a gypsy caravan
trailing clouds of dust ...
the vacant street

Hibiscus

Dawn is still a little way off. It is just a faint glow on the eastern horizon.
Walking past the shrubbery a twitter makes me stop to have a closer look. All
the plants are still silhouettes. The twitter is emanating from one of them.
Only a few days ago I had discovered a sunbird nest in the hibiscus. I had
gone to get some red hibiscus flowers for my offerings at the shrine but I could
see only a few yellowing leaves and some tender buds.

Is the bird-cheep coming from the sunbird nest? Suddenly there is a flutter
and the sunbird darts out. A thin golden line has begun to outline the clouds.
Feeling reassured I resume my walk.

spider's web
in the bare branches
a bit of sky

haibun

more ...

A fuller definition of each genre

HAIKU is a brief verse that epitomizes a single moment. It uses the juxtaposition of two concrete images, often a universal condition of nature and a particular aspect of human experience, in a way that prompts the reader to make an insightful connection between the two. The best haiku poems allude to the appropriate season of the year.

SENRYU, to quote Alan Pizarelli: "Senryu is a short poetic genre which focuses on people. It portrays the characteristics of human beings as well as the psychology of the human mind. The senryu can make use of poetic devices such as simile, personification, and metaphor. It can also employ puns, parody and satire. Unlike haiku, senryu are not reliant on a seasonal or nature reference. Senryu are not all strictly intended to be humorous. Many senryu express the misfortunes, the hardships and woe of humanity."

TANKA, the 5-line lyric poem of Japan is quickly becoming popular in the English-language poetry community. Like haiku, tanka usually is well-grounded in concrete images but also is infused with a lyric intensity and intimacy that comes from the direct expression of emotions, as well as from implication, suggestion, and nuance. The tanka aesthetic is broad and all-encompassing. One can write on virtually any subject and express thoughts and feelings explicitly.

HAIBUN is a prose that uses embedded haiku (or tanka) to enhance the composition's overall resonance and effect. Each verse (haiku or tanka) should be able to stand on its own as a poem, without repeating what is already in the prose, an interesting challenge in its own right.

*The definitions are taken from Alan Summers, *Decoding Tanka*, and *Writing Poetry: the haiku way*
*Alan Pizzarelli, author of numerous collections of haiku and senryu, is widely anthologized in major publications

afterword

by tracy koretsky

FIRST Katha book of haiku, senryu, tanka & haibun: a tour

1.

There's nothing like haiku to tell you just what a poet is thinking. So it would seem that, above all, the poets in this collection are thinking about rain! From Rohini Gupta's "light rain", with its downward gaze at a singular object to Narendra Kumar Dixit's "heavy downpour", with its upward gaze at the many, fifteen poems in all — more than any other subject or quality — dip umbrellas and share them, or observe the water buffalo. Interspersed as they are — as opposed to relegated to a seasonal arrangement as is often found in more traditional haiku anthologies — these poems run through the collection like a bass line, continually reminding the reader how much life in India is governed by its fierce monsoon.

While these poems show readers what the skies in India are like, it may be far more telling to note that in this collection, there are seven poems about breath. These show readers what the people are like.

Taken together, these poems offer an enticing glimpse of what this anthology holds in store.

For a start, there are no shortage of poems that revel in shear loveliness. Take this gorgeous piece by K Ramesh, a poet whose fine examples will suffuse this afterword:

> meditation over ...
> the full moon
> between the branches

In those psychically and spiritually open moments, when the meditation hasn't left you though you've had to move on, in those moments when you sense that your own energy still cloaks you, a vision of the moon — here so succinctly and perfectly stated — presents itself. The ellipsis, too, is well chosen, attenuating the line.

afterword

From that exquisitely heightened consciousness, to this shuddering corporeal observation by
S B Vadivelrajan:

> waterfall ...
> searching for my breath
> in the biting chill

to Shernaz Wadia's slightly surreal:

> this glassy lake
> of tranquility ...
> sitting at its edge
> with one breath
> I swallow the universe

to Kala Ramesh's sublimely lyric:

> longing
> for more, I linger ...
> a quiet breath
> over the widening blue
> of sea and sky

these wide-ranging poems never stray far from lovely.

And, between the breath and all that rain, to our delight, the universal: Chitra Rajappa's "sleeping
newborn"; Minal Sarosh's "old bones"; and R J Kalpana's "abandoned wheelchair" present images known
to all people. This quality is particularly well-captured in some of the senryu, like these by Seshu Chamarty
and Amitava Dasgupta respectively:

> ghost movie ...
> watched it again
> in my dream

business lunch
I will have
what the boss is having

These are the poems which have the capacity to make any people of any nation smile.

2.

FIRST Katha book of haiku, senryu, tanka & haibun is a collection very much in accord with contemporary international style. For example, not one of the poems is written in lines of 5/7/5 syllables. There are even a couple of two-line haiku — still considered avant-garde in many haiku circles — like this one from Kameshwar Rao:

pacing my steps
to a bird's morning call

in which the poet, through an act of will, brings himself into sync with nature. Notice that we are presented here with the action as it is ongoing; we are brought right into the moment. Another way in which this collection might be considered contemporary is the location of many of its kigo, the word or phrase in a haiku that is specific to a season. To demonstrate, observe this quiet moment sensually depicted by Harish Suryanarayana in which the kigo occupies its traditional position:

still winter night
the wind chimes tinkle
as I close the door

But in contemporary haiku, the kigo is not always on the first line. For example, where is the season word in this piece by Angelee Deodhar?

late for school
the green mangoes still
out of reach

afterword

Look for the word most specific to a particular time period. "School" spans most of the months of the year, so that might not be the best choice. On the other hand, the mangoes in line two will be green only briefly. That's the kigo.

Is a green mango ripe? Or not yet ripe? Are the kids starting the school year or finishing it? Their bodies/ the mangoes — are there similarities? By considering these various alternatives, a reader can appreciate the resonance of a well-selected kigo. And it is through considering these alternatives that the reader participates in the poem, thus unlocking its meaning.

It can be helpful when re-reading haiku to focus next on the last line. Why? Because the choices the poet makes in the second line are very much affected by its final one.

One strategy is like a cliffhanger: the second line suggests multiple outcomes then leaves off. These possibilities are resolved in line three. Some of the best third lines contain a surprise as in this poem by Kala Ramesh:

> autumn chill
> the ashtray holds
> their conversation

Since we expect cigarettes and that expectation is foiled, we smile. So getting to this third line, bringing us to the point where we absolutely must return after the commercial break, is the job of the second line. To see how N K Singh constructs his cliffhanger in this poem, stop at the end of the second line and envision all the surfaces that leaves might be tumbling upon:

> autumn …
> leaves tumble into

Go ahead; brainstorm a list. Now read the third line:

> a painter's palette

What a fine choice! Of all the choices he might have made, the poet has chosen to have the colors of nature fall upon the artist's medium. The tableau is thus completed with such a pretty and interesting image. Since artist's palettes are often leaf-like in shape, the poem is unified and satisfying — a second layer.

See how the first (usually one line) and second parts of the poem work together? Perhaps more than anything, this is the key to parsing haiku. The second part is not a definition of the first, not an expansion of its concept, nor is it a metaphor for it. Rather the parts work together much like two notes sounded at the same instant; the poem's meaning is an outcome of the overtones the notes create. Haiku requires active reading.

Finally, to address their subject matter: in a few brief lines, usually a phrase that can be uttered in just a single breath, the poet asks us to notice — merely that. Despite the cacophony and tumult that constantly demand our attention, we pause with the poet and attempt to direct our consciousness to a single moment before it flees.

Often that moment is brief and ephemeral. Srinjay Chakravarti's with his golden flash of an oriole's wings, Angelee Deodhar with her "wagtail dips" and "birdbath shivers", or Kala Ramesh's especially lovely dragonfly paused mid-glide are fine examples.

But beyond the goal of capturing an instant, the haiku poet strives to convey his or her experience of that moment, that is, the essential and personal experience. One goal for a haiku is that it translates, that somewhere in the world, in a place very different from where the poet lives, a reader is able to understand.

3.

That, above all, may be the richest gift this anthology offers. Here the reader is given a wide vantage. Twenty-two men and thirteen woman from everywhere in India, from every landscape, elucidate and share with us their culture in a way that only haiku can: with intensity and clarity.

In distinctive snapshots, Sunil Uniyal portrays his unforgettable guide twirling his moustache before the Delhi Red Fort, and Rohini Gupta, her temple left to its flowers. Some of the best of these are memorable due to their reliance on senses other than sight, such as the sound of the train in Kala Ramesh's "dense fog … " or this viscerally affecting piece by Bhavani Ramesh, with its evocative and disconcerting third line:

> sidewalk café
> I smell the city
> in my coffee

India is a land of many celebrations, and we are shown these too. Gautam Nadkarni flashes the intensity of Ganeshotsav and Diwali, while Charishma Ramchandani's vantage is more intimate. Perhaps though, it is the light shone upon the daily and personal celebrations, which provides deeper understanding for the foreign reader. In

> anniversary dinner
> we both order
> vegetarian

Amitava Dasgupta depicts a custom: one way to sanctify a meal, to give it reverence, is to eat vegetarian. Or here, in

> funeral procession
> a bee lands on the flowers

Johannes Manjrekar, with two brief lines, captures an entire belief system: the flowers upon the dead are, of course, themselves dead, but still capable vehicles for the continuation of life. The poem is especially deft because it is not explicit; it leaves the reader to contemplate its depth.

All together, the collection yields additional insights. It says something about a culture, for example, that there are many more poems here about religion than about war. Furthermore, from Gautam Nadkarni's "churchyard" to K. Ramesh's "vedic chants", many different types of religion are referred to, more frequently than not, merely as backdrops for other dramas.

But of those poems about war, this one is particularly striking:

> rumours of war
> up into a darkening sky
> — a child's newsprint kite

Here, Angelee Deodhar ties to the end of a child's arm all the things that kites mean: a toy dictated by wind, its tenuous attachment nevertheless forceful, something that could break away, out of control, or stall and land, perhaps hopelessly entangled. But not just a kite, a kite constructed of news of the day, gray with distance, which happens to threaten of war, its potential pull upon the child, ominous, as unstoppable as wind. Not surprisingly, this poem once won Third Prize in the prestigious Robert Spiess Memorial Haiku Award.

A similar tension is at work in poems like Usha Kiran's celebration of a power outage:

> power cut ...
> today I hear
> the birds chirp

and A Thiagarajan's

> mid-may
> the narielwala walks across
> for a cold coke

in which the vendor of a refreshing and traditional coconut drink foregoes his own wares. In these, we sense the disquiet of a culture undergoing rapid change.

4.

Perhaps more than anything though, what gives this collection its unique voice is its fullness. It brims with crowded tableaux, with rich and complicated music, yet with lovely and clear image.

We can see this, for example, in the depiction of people, almost always, shown multiply, sometimes, as

afterword

crowds. But even when not in crowds, people are, for the most part, cited in the plural. Kumarendra Mallick has not chosen a single child to occlude his shadow in his "morning walk" but multiple. Or, here in

> sound of waves …
> a jogger stops to watch
> the fishermen leave

one person, the poet, K Ramesh, watches another person, a jogger who stops to watch, not one but many, people.

Even when a single individual owns the poet's gaze, other people seem to block the view, as in Gautam Nadkarni's:

> smiling back I find
> that the girl is smiling
> at someone else

A scene re-enacted in every city on every moment of every day, and so, a universal senryu.

It is interesting to note that this poem by A Sethuramiah:

> between me
> and the mountain range
> a train passes

was published in the Mainichi Daily news, the English language edition of Japan's oldest — and one of its most popular — newspapers. The poem depicts a scene that would likely strike a common chord with a Japanese reader. But unlike Japan, there seems at times to be no landscape that is not peopled, no privacy, where true aloneness can be complete. Take this very striking poem by Usha Kiran:

> toilet …
> smell of freshly fried papad
> from our neighbour's kitchen

in which the sweetly delicious scent from a near-by kitchen causes her to salivate. Not for a single moment is the poet able to untangle from web of her community.

We see this again and again in the haibun and haiga of Johannes Manjrekar who uses it to great expressive effect depicting multiple, complex interpersonal relationships, each a cinematic drama, fraught yet reported without judgment. His fascinating haiga "Afternoon", especially bears repeated scrutiny. In a scene packed with competing pattern and movement from the abutting designs of the women's saris to the blurred motorbike riders, only the grainy surface provides visual unity. The poem, with its reference to the Muslim call to prayer, evokes a soundscape, while offering both a type of peace and the ladder to get there.

Now, not only are these poems packed with people, but many depict people in close proximity to large animals: camels, cows, or, as in this poem by Srinjay Chakravarti, water buffalo:

> monsoon clouds ...
> a herd of water buffalo
> wades into the pond

Notice that its kigo is plural as are the buffalo — everything in quantity.

We, each of us, have, in our own mind's eye, an image of monsoon clouds. We then place within it a herd of water buffalo. What about them? What will they do? The third line resolves this by giving them an action. It is an action — moving towards safety before the storm — that we hope our poet is doing at that very moment, expressing his oneness with the natural world.

The ellipsis is a strong choice here allowing time to lapse as the water buffalo prepare for the storm. Serendipity perhaps, but there is also a delightful concrete aspect to this choice, like a row of clouds along the top line. Like all of the poems featuring animals in this collection, this poem conveys strongly a sense of place, one of the virtues of good haiku.

Several poems rejoice in the peace and preciousness of being alone — another way to underscore its rarity. Surprisingly though, even within that revelry, the poet seeks to join other beings. We see this

afterword

in the emotional call to the gypsies in Vidur Jyoti's movingly lonely haibun "Are You There?"; in the personification of the tree in Purushothama Rao's "spring rain" — the tree an active participant, one player in the drama; or in Puja Malusht's "autumn dusk", in which her waiting is a sentient presence. K Ramesh, in particular, is effective in portraying this yearning aloneness, making the subject of several poems his awareness that he is in the presence of others, be they stars, or even just a little bug lost to its struggle.

5.

These are poems not just full of people; they are full in every sense. Consider the Indian garland: every surface, 360 degrees, a carpet of blooms. Now look again at these poems. Note, for example, Vidur Jyoti's "first rains". Why "rains" and not "rain"? Because, so often here, the poets choose plurals, choose fullness. And see how it operates psychologically? Many rains is a heavier emotional realization. These are the first moments of many rains to come and the poet's response is to care for, or at least, to reach for, someone else.

Here's another way to see this attribute at work: R J Kalpana's

> high noon —
> by the car a girl stands
> on her shadow

Observe how the reader's attention is moved here. We have high (up), by (next to) and "on." The prepositions are indicative of a consciousness that takes in and assumes concurrent movement and multiple directions: a fullness of tableau.

Look at this poem by R K Singh:

> Making lemon tea
> and warm buttery toast —
> birds singing outside

We have here not just tea, but bright yellow lemon tea, not just toast, but warm buttery-yellow toast, and the birds, as expressed by continuous present verb in line 3, singing even now. The fullness of this piece is the very thing that makes it cozy.

Even the preference for British spelling, with its many vowels, as in Usha Kiran's "leaving home", or Johannes Manjrekar's haibun contributes a typographic fullness. Listen too, to this line from Aju Mukhopadhyay's haibun "Crickets Drone": Droning of crickets we often hear

This is the music of English as spoken by Indians, the lulling rhythms of which inflect so many of these poems. See how it works in this one from Johannes Manjrekar:

> rumble of thunder
> a sunbird comes darting
> through the wire fence

An alternative second line might have been "a sunbird darts" though what would have been lost, besides its rhythmic pattern, was the continuation of the um/un rhyme scheme before the poem gives over to its "r" sounds.

These are poems exquisitely conscious of language, their diction, painstakingly selected. Consider Sunil Uniyal's "heckled", Vishnu P Kapoor's "frisky" — so much expressed in the single verb or adjective. Many of these poems operate on language — turn on it. By the end of line two of one of Angelee Deodhar's poems she is "arrested by a shock" at an exit. What can this mean in our dangerous world? But then a secondary meaning of "arrested' comes into play as in "a capturing of attention," and by what? By the most open and friendly of flowers. Wit.

Another sort of wit is demonstrated in the several concrete poems, such as Reshma Jain's "blurry sonograph", Devika Menon's "summer sunset", and R J Kalpana's "floundering boat", which indent their second lines.

This one:

> bored in heaven
> a shooting star
> jumps to death

by Raju Samal, also makes use of personification as do Purushothama Rao's "spring rain", and Sunil Uniyal's "the mist is heavy" — still another kind of wit.

And if all this wit isn't fun enough for you, then listen to the music of these poems:

Note the rhyme scheme created by between/me - you/moon in Puja Malushte's "twilight", or the pattern created by the long vowel pulsing through G S P Rao's poem "autumn deepens", before releasing into the graceful final line with its soft vowel.

Not only is there rhyme, but skillful rhythm as well. For example, in Puja Malushte's "autumn dusk", the implied punctuation is "me, and my waiting". The poet has subtly embedded commas into her rhythm.

Why, Rohini Gupta's "cloud shadow" could even, with only the slightest force, be read as iambic. In another poem by this fine ear poet:

> light rain
> the red rose
> overflows

The word "red" prevents the poem from becoming sing-song. Instead, the rhyme is retained but with the added alliteration of red and rain, a more complex pattern emerges.

It is not always true that haiku in English fully utilizes the sounds available in its language. But in this collection it is true — abundantly so.

6.

Abundance. That is perhaps the one word that best describes this important harvest of poems. And yet, paradoxically, fascinatingly, these are poems that gird their profusion into five lines or fewer, into time spans no longer than a blink. Distilled they are piquant, gathered they are the temptations of a thali dinner.

From snow pack to swelter, from the middle of the night until glaring noon, from silver fish obliterating diaries to camels adjudicating arguments, from droning crickets to thunderclaps to the exceeding slow beat of a vilambit teen tal, the first anthology of Indian haiku, senryu, tanka and haibun is part Baedeker, part family photo album, part sacred text, and all symphony, every player essential to its enthralling music. Listen again.

ACKNOWLEDGEMENTS

I would like to thank Geeta for all the encouragement she gave for the unfolding of this book. Now, when I think back, what strikes me is her forethought and vision.

My heartfelt gratitude to my co-editors, Johannes Manjrekar and Vidur Jyoti, for their patience and critical awareness of what constitutes a haiku, a senryu, a tanka and a haibun. It is certainly not easy. Given their job demands, it is nothing short of a miracle that they found time for voting and discussing the selections at every juncture.

My special thanks to each editor and designer of the Katha team, who initially worked so hard to put this up as an ebook in 2013. Thanks to the editor Neha Gupta for working with me for this print edition. I love the dream spaces they have given throughout the book. To Surabhi Singh, my special thanks for the lovely illustrations.

I would like to thank Tracy Koretsky, who has done such a wonderful job, analysing each poem and giving us, as far as possible, an exhaustive summary. This book would have been so incomplete had she not agreed to pitch in with her views and reviews.

To all our readers, to the initiated and the uninitiated, welcome to the world of haiku and its related genres. You won't be disappointed, for sure! In 2009 this was the best that India could offer and many of these poems were published throughout the whole wide world, from England to Japan, online and in anthologies. A special thanks to all those editors sitting in far-flung corners of the world who saw beauty, immediacy and that simple but striking imagery in our work, which should elicit that Wah and applause from you, dear rasika.

For this anthology, Johannes Manjrekar, Vidur Jyoti and I carefully went through over six hundred poems and, through blind voting, meticulously selected 154 beautiful poems including haiku, senryu, tanka, and haibun for your reading pleasure.

These poems were selected in October 2009, and were published as an ebook by Katha in 2013. Since then, haikai literature has lured many Indian enthusiasts into its fold, and they are doing exceptionally well in the world haiku scene. I honestly regret that their lovely poems could not be included in this print edition Katha is bringing out for young adults. Hoping Katha soon sends out a call for the SECOND anthology of haikai poetry!

Kala Ramesh
Pune

BIONOTES

Kala Ramesh writes haiku, tanka, haibun, senryu and renku. Anthologised in Haiku 21: an anthology of contemporary English-language haiku (Modern Haiku Press, 2012) and Haiku in English — the First Hundred Years (W W Norton, 2013). Kala's initiatives over the years culminated in founding "INhaiku" on 23rd of February at the Haiku Utsav 2013, primarily to get Indian haikai poets under one umbrella — to promote, enjoy and sink deeper into the beauty and intricacies of this art form.

Johannes Manjrekar grew up mostly in Mysore, Karnataka. His education consisted largely of insect collecting, bird-watching and swimming, supplemented eventually by a Ph.D. in molecular biology from the Tata Institute of Fundamental Research, Mumbai. Since 1989, he's been teaching M.Sc. students in Microbiology and Biotechnology at Baroda's M.S. University. Apart from haikai, he is very enthusiastic about photography.

Vidur Jyoti, a surgeon by training, took to writing at an early stage during his student career and later on diversified into writing short essays and verse which saw him being guided to haiku and related genre. He has a keen interest in philosophy and culture. He regards his professional activities as an opportunity for an insight into life almost a meditational experience to be shared with everyone in verse and prose. His haiku, tanka and other writings appear in some anthologies published from India and abroad.

Tracy Koretsky writes and publishes across genres, from haiku to novel, from literary criticism to screenplay, ever fascinated by their nuances and the intersections between them. Witness this yourself in her memoir in poems, Even before my own name, (www.TracyKoretsky.com) which she invites you to download with her compliments.

Ms. Koretsky is also the author of three novels: "Ropeless", (www. ReadRopeless.com) a 15-time, award-winning family drama that celebrates possibilities despite disabilities; "The Body of Helen," a backstage drama inspired by modern dancer, Martha Graham; and "The Novel of the Century," a romantic comedy about the importance of love, books, and choosing both. Her widely-published shorter work has earned more than fifty awards including three Pushcart Prize nominations.

ABOUT KATHA

Set up in 1988, Katha is a profit-for-all organization that works in the areas of education, publishing and community development. Working with and in story and storytelling since 1988, Katha is one of India's top publishing houses. Focusing on quality translations – our list includes more than 300 of India's best literary talents from twenty one languages – we showcase contemporary Indian fiction like no other publisher. Katha also introduces an array of writings from the many oral and written traditions of Indian to children, ages 0 – 17. Classy productions, child-friendly layouts and superb illustrations go in tandem with excellent writing.

OUR MISSION: Enhancing the joys of reading

OUR BELIEF: Stories help create friendships of a rare kin to culture link people, faiths and creative impulses. Stories are the life-savers of future nations.

OUR CREDO: An uncommon education for a common good

Katha stands as an exemplar for all the creative projects around the world that grapple with ordinary and dramatic misery in cities.
— **Charles Landry, The Art of City Making**

Katha has a real soft corner for kids. Which is why it … create[s] such gorgeous picture books for children. — **Time Out**

Katha … by establishing Reading Campaigns, re-education and culturelinking … has made a difference! — **Aghoo Review**

It is small in size, but don't let that fool you. — **Haiku, G R LeBlanc, Canadian Blogger**

… tugs at your imagination … — **I Have a Home, Parenting**

… the dearly loved world of Tagore. — **Katha Bangla Library, The Open Library**

This delectable book, like a chocolate ice-cream, is for all ages, moods and minds. And as for the price – well, it's Priceless!
— **On the Tip of a Pin Was, bolokids.com**

A wonderful attempt to bring such folk art in prominence.
— **Bioscope, Literary Sojourn**

Singh shows how many facets of his professional being – grammarian, linguist, translator, wordsmith, poet – come together to celebrate his unbridled lust for written words. Listen to the first few lines of Leave a little space: "Leave a little space for me. I'm a poet."
— **Second Person Singular, Harmony Magazine**

about katha

grab another book on

haiku

from katha's library

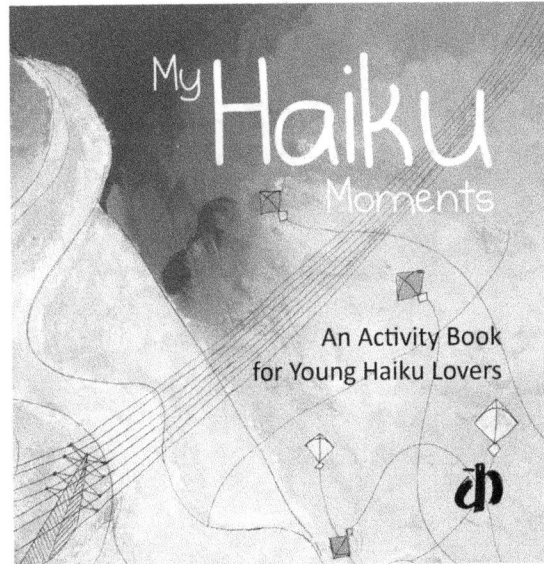

HAIKU AND A COMPANION ACTIVITY BOOK

Kala Ramesh | Art by Surabhi Singh

Here's a lovely compilation of evocative Haiku poems that will light up your child's vibrant imagination. The interactive three-dimensional book is fun to hold and read. Comes with an exciting and engaging activity book replete with detailed explanations and examples. A must have for all the young poets and their teachers!

It's whimsical, it's colourful and it gives a spin to poetry in motion. The tiny square book unfolds to reveal beautiful illustrations. The book is accompanied by My Haiku Moments, an activity book in which children can compose their own poems. The guide offers tips and sets of exercises for the readers, making it a great gift.

— **Time Out**

must haves for
nature lovers

Written in a manner that children will understand, it is sure to wake the little environmentalist within them.

— **Kidsstoppress**

A TREE
Klara Köttner-Benigni
Art by Tribal Artists from India

One poet and twelve tribal storytellers, some of India's most loved illustrators! They encourage you to — Think. Ask questions. Discuss and then swing into ACTION as an Earth-Carer!

Recommended for The Leading Reading Schools of India Award, organized by Young India Books

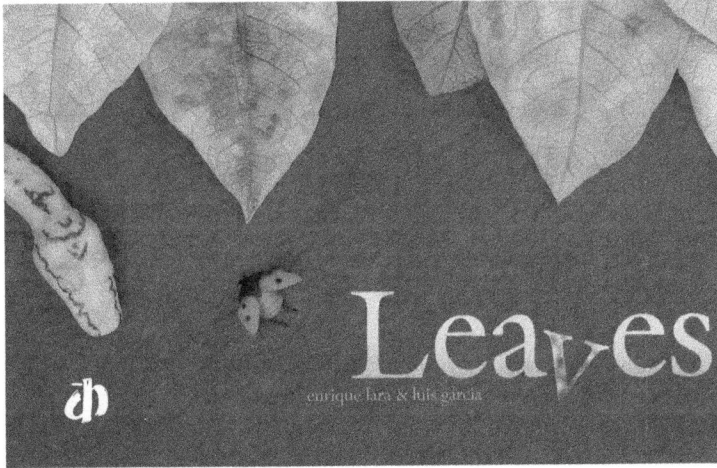

LEAVES

Enrique Lara Robayo and Luis Fernando Garcia Guayara

"From the window of my room I see amazing things ..." A book that can be read and enjoyed by everyone from the very young to the old!

Leaves zooms into the colour and magic of nature.
— **Young World, The Hindu**

THE MYNA FROM PEACOCK GARDEN

Naiyer Masud | Art by Premola Ghose

Translated from the Urdu

Work is on in full swing at the Royal Peacock Garden to install a wondrous cage that will house forty talking hill mynas. Soon, the cage and its lively, twittering occupants are entrusted to Kale Khan's care. But he steals a myna for his little motherless daughter, who has long been asking him for one. What lies in store for Kale Khan ... and the beautiful historic city of Lucknow?

... [a] masterful portrayal of the Lucknow of yore.
— **The World of Urdu Poetry**

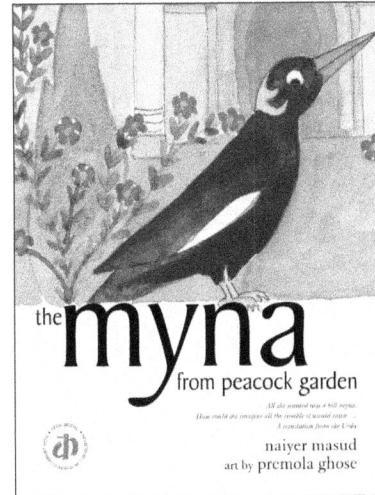

www.ingramcontent.com/pod-product-compliance
Lightning Source LLC
LaVergne TN
LVHW061305060426
835513LV00013B/1250